Unsung Offerings

poems by

Marianne Brems

Finishing Line Press
Georgetown, Kentucky

Unsung Offerings

Copyright © 2021 by Marianne Brems
ISBN 978-1-64662-607-6 First Edition
All rights reserved under International and Pan-American Copyright Conventions. No part of this book may be reproduced in any manner whatsoever without written permission from the publisher, except in the case of brief quotations embodied in critical articles and reviews.

ACKNOWLEDGMENTS

"Unsung Offerings" and "Flower Stems" appeared in *The Fictional Café* August 18, 2019
"The Ghost of Mazama" and "Glacial Shapes" appeared in *Willows Wept* June 20, 2020
"Seven Seconds" appeared in *Academy of the Heart and Mind* October 30, 2019
"An Old Blue Oak" appeared in *The Pangolin Review* September 8, 2018
"Sunflowers" appeared in *Fleas on the Dog* May 15, 2020
"Night Sky" appeared in *Soft Cartel* June 8, 2018
"A Treelike Shape" appeared in *Academy of the Heart and Mind* January 2019 "Their Ritual" and "All in a Line" appeared in *Academy of the Heart and Mind* May 9, 2020
"The Owl on the Fence" appeared in *Door is a Jar* Winter 2017
"A Reptilian Time Machine" appeared in *Armarolla* October 11, 2018
"Somewhere a Bluebird Trills" appeared in *Trestle Ties* July 1, 2020

Publisher: Leah Huete de Maines
Editor: Christen Kincaid
Cover Art: Ricardo Gomez Angel via unsplash.com
Author Photo: Joan Bresnan
Cover Design: Elizabeth Maines McCleavy

Order online: www.finishinglinepress.com
also available on amazon.com

Author inquiries and mail orders:
Finishing Line Press
PO Box 1626
Georgetown, Kentucky 40324
USA

Table of Contents

Unsung Offerings 1

Seven Seconds 2

An Old Blue Oak 3

Mud Creek Landslide 4

Sunflowers 5

The Ghost of Mazama 6

Night Sky 7

Glacial Shapes 8

Displacement 9

Bright Colors 10

Flower Stems 11

A Treelike Shape 12

Their Ritual 13

All in a Line 14

Traces 15

A Jar Full of Sea Air 16

The Owl on the Fence 17

A Reptilian Time Machine 18

These Ants with their Burdens 19

Living with Loathing 20

The Need for Salt 21

Somewhere a Bluebird Trills 22

For Joan

Introduction

The natural world holds an infinite number of captivating unexamined aspects and tiny everyday vignettes often overlooked. It is the purpose of this collection to draw attention to a few of these so that readers may come away with a new sense of connection between the many seemingly disparate things in our living environment.

Unsung Offerings

Dandelion leaves like lions' teeth
turn up everywhere
with yellow faces like champions in their midst
serving spring nectar to hungry pollinators.
They show up early and stay late,
then depart sending fluffy parachutes
off in the wind to new venues.

Not idle guests,
their taproots pull up nutrients
that fertilize grass.
When consumed, they ease muscle aches,
joint pain, digestive distress, and more.
Their roots loosen hard soil,
aerate the earth, reduce erosion.
They handle their own planting.
Their every cell is edible.
And they're sturdy as a girder.

These lions' teeth
with their unsung offerings
come from seeds we never see.
They reach.
They grow.
They work for free
though so many perish
in a hateful reign of annihilation
with hoe and trowel.

Seven Seconds

A leaf separates from a twig on a tree
tumbling for seven seconds
on a journey to the ground.

For seven seconds a pedestrian
crosses a busy intersection
before a swarm of traffic invades.

A mother sparrow satisfies hunger
as she drops insects for seconds
into the gaping beaks of her young.

A concert master stands, baton poised,
head raised for large seconds
before sweet sound spreads.

A pause stretches for seven seconds
before a first kiss
felt as far as the soles of eager feet.

With the fragrance of eucalyptus
passing through my window,
seconds stroll lightly by
as a leaf quietly comes to rest.

An Old Blue Oak

Not as old as the Civil War, but close.
A Blue Oak spreads its twisted arms
around a loving sky,
arms decayed from the senseless violations
of humans
with their digging machines that sever roots
and their trucks that belch forth concrete.

Arms that care in spite of it all
and fight for the life bestowed.
Arms that push forth a canopy of green
that shades the heads of the guilty.
Arms that also reach the ground,
embracing it, palms up,
with lichen covered fingers
and stalks of nascent grass
that unfold to take them in.

Mud Creek Landslide

At the moment of her choosing,
    a thousand tons of saturated earth
        rumble down the cliff,
            burying the highway below,
                and emptying itself at last into the sea.

But not right after the rains.
She waits a month or two
to think it over first,
to tactically plan the maneuver.
Seventy-five acres of land displaced
in the blink of an eye.
A shoreline reshaped
like an apron.
A smooth sheet of rubble with no cut
for a road full of craning onlookers.
A statement as bold as a blood stain
with wisps of fog bowing in deference.

Now this earth mother
    calculates just when movement should recede,
        when to allow construction to pick up the pieces
            to try to make order of her formidable handiwork
                so decisively laid before the feet of the ocean.

Sunflowers

Like a magnet, the sun draws
the young faces of sunflowers
east in the morning,
west in the evening,
back again at night,
expectant of the dawn.
A biomass hungry for sunshine
to offer a warm landing
for bees.

In gratitude
nodding golden heads migrate.
Yellow follows yellow,
paying tribute
to a benevolent source
of nurture
fluttering down
from the protective canopy
of a parental sky.

The Ghost of Mazama

The Rim Road around Crater Lake
with a dusting of snow beside it
is nearly all mine.
In temporal sunlight
I ride on two slim tires
around a lake without tributaries,
deeper than a skyscraper.

My core swells in warmth
pushing heat out my arms
as I ascend,
receding again during descent
when fierce wind imposes.
The swing from one to the other
like a trapeze as Watchman Outlook
nods in acknowledgment.

Where glacial blue and shale gray meet
below a thin white blanket,
I am a tiny traveler
following a concrete cut
in the pine dotted flank
of once molten Mount Mazama.

As the autumn sun passes midday,
a forest ready to host hibernation,
lures me on
around this ancient caldera,
the ghost of Mazama
hovering near my sternum.

Night Sky

Far from the city lights,
the night sky is endless.
Without glimmering towers or
a distant swell of urban radiance
to punctuate the blackness,
it blends seamlessly into the horizon,
no delicate membrane
or shift in texture
to separate the two,
a limitless shadow it seems,
though of course it isn't so.
Shadows cover halves of things
while the other halves stay bright.
Darkness without counter light
withers with indifference,
incomplete,
like Yin without Yang.

Glacial Shapes

The giants,
Everest,
Half Dome,
Dents du Midi,
speak in booming voices,
chests protruding,
to announce their immensity
as distant visitors gape
then huddle so cameras can snap
before greater wonders
overtake.

Yet nestled among these looming titans
are smaller shapes
too numerous to name,
rocky serpents rising from a sea of shale,
or galloping horsemen anchored in place;
anonymous glacially sculpted creations
never darkened by a footprint
who speak through softer edges
and quieter voices
to reflective observers,
no cameras in hand.

Displacement

Where does this cavity go that fits me precisely
when I exit the ocean?
No even exchange of atmosphere
for an equal volume of water when I leave.
Vestiges of me still fill space.

Trace molecules of my
sodium,
potassium,
carbon dioxide,
expired epidermal cells,
mingled with my volition
to move through the waves,
names forgotten of places I used to go,
sediment from scrapes against cliffs
that crumble when touched,
all clenched in the ocean's memory of me.

Bright Colors

Days dawn,
nights unfold,
cliffs erode,
and glaciers melt
mostly without notice.

In the meantime,
cancers grow,
deadlines pass,
divorces proceed,
and checks bounce.

We maintain as we
don wedding rings
lift grandchildren,
clean closets,
and wear bright colors.

Flower Stems

If heaven were a place
to walk without fear of an audience
jaded in judgement,
a place to love without concern
for running alone on earth's curve,
a place to rise in the morning
without tripping on stones by evening,
a place to play in rushing rivers
without risk of being swept away,
a place to carry wood to a fire
that never burns out,
a place to throw out regrets
with the dust swirls of empty rooms,

a place where traffic lights are all green,
the sun always sets peacefully after dinner,
and sleeves are never too short,

then resilience would wither,
muscles atrophy,
bones relinquish density
in a field where flowers fill every space
and their stems, though succulent,
make the sturdiest pillars.

A Treelike Shape

An elderly Blue Oak
stands intact
with bark that hugs her girth,
photosynthesis
coursing through her veins,
sculpting the air around her
into a temple for her soul.

Were she to crumble and collapse,
atmosphere in her shape
would fill the cavern,
space would slide through
where phloem once was,
substance would mourn the loss
of tracheids and vessels,
content to cherish the heartbeat
of a still lasting goddess.

Their Ritual

Sparrows prance on slick rock
where water bubbles
down from a fountain.
They primp
and fluff
and puff their dripping chests.
They wet their heads
and rub them clean
with the undersides of wings.
They peck
and chase
and squawk at each other,
their energy focused like a spear
as they jostle to claim the territory
to best perform their ritual.

All in a Line

Geese know just the line
to cheat the wind.
Each falls in line
like days of the week
to ease the burden behind.
Strong ones,
weak ones,
all of one mind
while drivers below
crawl along in steel cocoons,
all in a line,
and feast on their rage,
blind to the birds
as they vent at each other
for going just too damn slow.

Traces

Like a single ray of sunlight caught in a crystal,
wings that swing for thousands of miles
distil into tiny footprints in the sand
each a roadmap of foraging and nurturing
within an ever-changing landscape.

From the hint of pollen clinging to a bee
gorging on luscious nectar,
a goldenrod full and vibrant comes to life,
its yellow crown claiming a fertile space
within an ever-changing landscape.

A miniscule grain of sand in an oyster's mantel,
vexing as a splinter,
draws layer upon layer of soothing nacre
birthing in its wake an iridescent gem
within an ever-changing landscape.

A Jar Full of Sea Air

A jar full of sea air
opened in a meadow
dampens a small corner of sunlight
that blossoms with its treasure
joining sea and land together
in perfect union.

The Owl on the Fence

She sits with focused purpose.
Her tail is long, too long.
Her head bobs slightly with the breeze,
an odd movement.
The rest of her is still, too still.
She lingers longer than I expect.
But I believe her.
I think she is a living breathing warrior.

Yet to deceive is her one ambition.
She has no blood, no bones, nor stomach,
no hunter's vision of mice and squirrels.
Hollow she sits,
a coquette of sorts,
to convince birds
danger lies within her lifeless beak.

What need has she of a heart and lungs
when vacant plastic is enough?
We the deceived, the birds and I,
with our protoplasmic brains
provide no match for her clever ways.

A Reptilian Time Machine

A rabbit poses no match for the turtle.
This we learned as toddlers.
But it's not about the race,
though time is a factor.

Time turns a clever corner
when turtle temperature drops.
In the pond's muddy underworld,
heartrate recedes
to one beat in minutes.
Breathing moves to the tail
and nearly stops.
Digestion slows to a halt.
Meanwhile negligible senescence,
a further hitch in time,
leaves even centenarian organs
untouched by age's decline.

Should wonder need a further nudge,
remember the house the turtle wears,
a weight she drags cross field and pond
but makes a home anywhere
for infinity and beyond.

So while the rabbit smugly snoozes,
our hearts stay rooted further on
with this reptilian time machine,
a creature of divine invention,
her carapace, her plastron,
and everything in between
built to sweeten the morsels of time
as they mellow and deepen.

These Ants with their Burdens

Ants scurry around my feet
schlepping tubes like tiny rigatoni.
Oh, the energy to move these burdens
two or three times their own length.

But their movement has
precision, purpose, grace.
Many participate in these formations
never faltering in the humble pursuit
to serve their community unit.

They soldier on,
cooperating as nest mates,
to build, to feed, to protect
the cavities, tributaries, and residents
of their rigatoni palace.

No fences around property,
no locks on their doors,
no backs turned on neighbors,
just the tireless transport of large masses
for the welfare of all.

Living with Loathing

Without conscience or concern,
we loathe snakes,
those sinuous shadowy reptiles
with their serpentine ways,
their presumed pernicious venom,
and their textured coverings
like faded oriental rugs,
their every movement
perceived as danger;
an affront to decent sensibility.

Yet we pay incidental tribute
to the leopard or the lynx,
equally aggressive warriors,
but whose elegance
revokes repugnance.

If snakes could run on fluid legs
or preen their glossy coat,
they would, of course, we say,
wouldn't they?

Though what choice have they
without beauty or grace
but to slither us into terror,
suffer unjust loathing,
and stick their tongues out at us?

The Need for Salt

A simple molecule of salt
becomes remarkable
once inside the body of an ibex.
It knows just where to go
to stimulate muscles and nerves
that control dexterous pincer-like moves
needed to scale nearly vertical rock walls.
Cleft sucker-padded feet spread wide
to cling to the tiniest outcroppings,
able to move their slim nimble bodies
up or down the sheerest face.

A simple block of mineral rich stone
becomes essential
when placed just so into the160-foot wall
of Italy's Cingino Dam.
It builds a lake for water and hydroelectricity,
its dissolved mineral salts,
the ultimate prize for the ibex
who climb to dizzying heights
to lick the salt that feeds their need.

Salt and stone.
Stone and salt.
Without them, each host cannot thrive.

Somewhere a Bluebird Trills

I sit in an over-used waiting room,
my chair with a crack in its black vinyl covering.
Faint smells of rubber and exhaust permeate.
Cosmopolitan two months old,
Newsweek from three weeks ago
that no one touches.

Television grabbing at me
from the ceiling in the corner,
controls out of reach,
no remote.
Volume loud enough to steal silence,
annihilate peace,
but too muted to project news or weather
or headache remedy.

I'm caught mid-flight in a web of
words without import
in a room without hush
where no one speaks
or watches or listens to
this desensitizing machine,
phones or laptops preferable,
while somewhere far away a bluebird trills.

Marianne Brems has an MA in Creative Writing from San Francisco State University. She is a long time writer of nonfiction and her publications include textbooks in her teaching area of English as a Second Language and several trade books. She began writing poetry in mid-life to capture essence and order in random events of daily life. She has a special interest in writing poems that exhibit a strong sense of the natural world. She is the author of the chapbook *Sliver of Change* (Finishing Line Press 2020). Her poems have also appeared in several literary journals including *The Pangolin Review, Armarolla, Nightingale & Sparrow, Scarlet Leaf Review, La Scrittrice, Willows Wept, Tiny Seed Literary Journal,* and *The Sunlight Press.* She lives in Northern California. Website: www.mariannebrems.com.

www.ingramcontent.com/pod-product-compliance
Lightning Source LLC
LaVergne TN
LVHW040118080426
835507LV00041B/1720